RELAXING

Flower Design

and Encouraging Quotes

for new

MOM

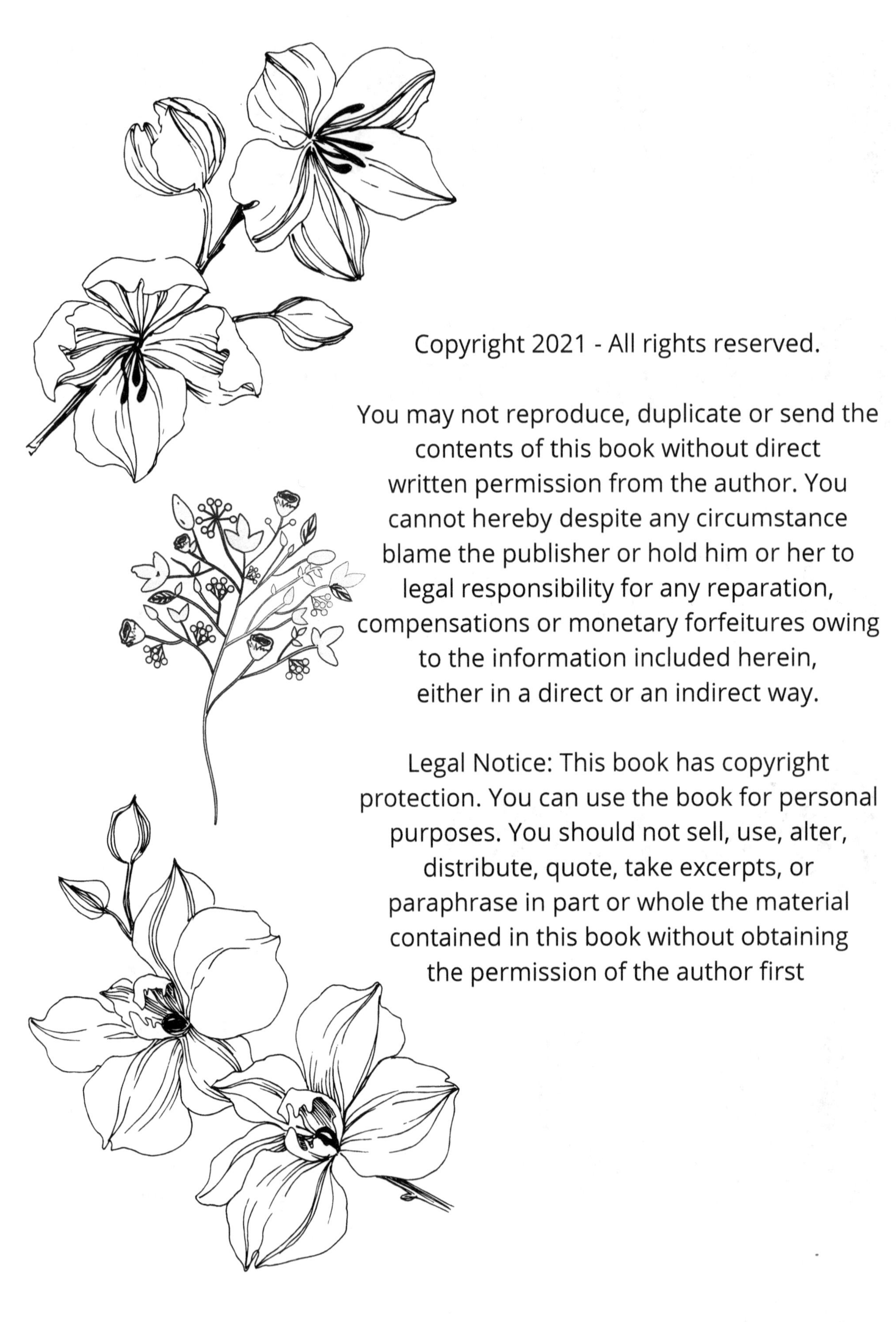

"There's no way to be a perfect mother and a million ways to be a good one."

"A baby will make love stronger, days shorter, nights longer, bankroll smaller, home happier, clothes shabbier, the past forgotten, and the future worth living for."

"When you are a mother, you are never really alone in your thoughts. A mother always has to think twice, once for herself and once for her child."

"I like to think of motherhood as a great big adventure. You set off on a journey, you don't really know how to navigate things, and you don't exactly know where you're going or how you're going to get there."

"Motherhood is the biggest gamble in the world. It is the glorious life force. It's huge and scary—it's an act of infinite optimism."

"The moment a child is born, the mother is also born. She never existed before. The woman existed, but the mother, never. A mother is something absolutely new."

"A baby is something you carry inside you for nine months, in your arms for three years and in your heart till the day you die."

"Making the decision to have a child is momentous. It is to decide forever to have your heart go walking around outside your body."

"A mother is always the beginning. She is how things begin."

"Giving birth and being born brings us into the essence of creation, where the human spirit is courageous and bold and the body, a miracle of wisdom."

"There is such a special sweetness in being able to participate in creation."

"Motherhood:
All love
begins and
ends there."

"Birthing is the most profound initiation to spirituality a woman can have."

"Of all the rights of women, the greatest is to be a mother."

"Sometimes the strength of motherhood is greater than natural laws."

"Birth takes a woman's deepest fears about herself and shows her that she is stronger than them".

"The natural state of motherhood is unselfishness. When you become a mother, you are no longer the center of your own universe. You relinquish that position to your children."

"There are hard days in motherhood. But looking at your sleeping baby reminds you why it's all worth it."

"Being a mother is the most rewarding blessing in the world. Just knowing you can love someone so much and get that same love in return is wonderful."

"Successful mothers are not the ones that have never struggled. They are the ones that never give up, despite the struggles."

"Having kids—the responsibility of rearing good, kind, ethical, responsible human beings—is the biggest job anyone can embark on."

"Your dream came true, your very own little one, your brand new life as a mother is about to begin. The moment you breathe in that new baby smell, you'll feel a love so fiercely, it's like nothing you've ever felt before."

"You're doing a great job,
mom, even when you
don't feel like it."

"God could not
be everywhere,
and therefore
he made
mothers."

"Mother: the
most beautiful
word on the
lips of
mankind."

"Take heart tired momma. You will make it through these exhausting days, and you will be stronger for them. You are a good mother. You only need to look into the eyes of your children and believe it."

"Motherhood: The only place you can experience Heaven and Hell at the same time."

"Becoming a mother makes you realize you can do almost anything one-handed."

Mother... a mother holds her
child's hand for just a short time
but holds their hearts forever.

"Life doesn't
come with a
manual, it
comes with a
mother."

"A baby fills a place in your heart
that you never knew was empty."

"Your dream came true, your very own little one, your brand new life as a mother is about to begin. The moment you breathe in that new baby smell, you'll feel a love so fierce, it's like nothing you've ever felt before."

"You will never have this day with your children again tomorrow. They will be a little older than they were today. This day is a gift just breathe and notice, smell and touch them, study their faces and little feet, pay attention, relish the charm of the present. Enjoy today."

"Great parenting happens when you start controlling yourself and stop controlling your child."

"Hey, mama. I see you stressed out, tired, touched out, stretched thin, irritable, snappy, imperfect, short-tempered, grumpy, crying, it's okay. Everybody has been there; it sucks, but you are good. You are a good mom, say it, believe it."

"Hold on to the tiny moments and cherish the little snuggles. They grow up so fast."

"Hold him a little longer, rock him a little more, read him another story, let him sleep on your shoulder. Rejoice in his happy smile; he is only a little boy for such a little while."

"To be motherly means to be both strong and nurturing."

"Motherhood is a million little moments that God weaves together with grace, redemption, laughter, tears, and most of all, love."

"Behind every great child
is a mom who's pretty sure
she's screwing it all up."

"The sweet smell of a baby must be one of the best smells in the whole world."

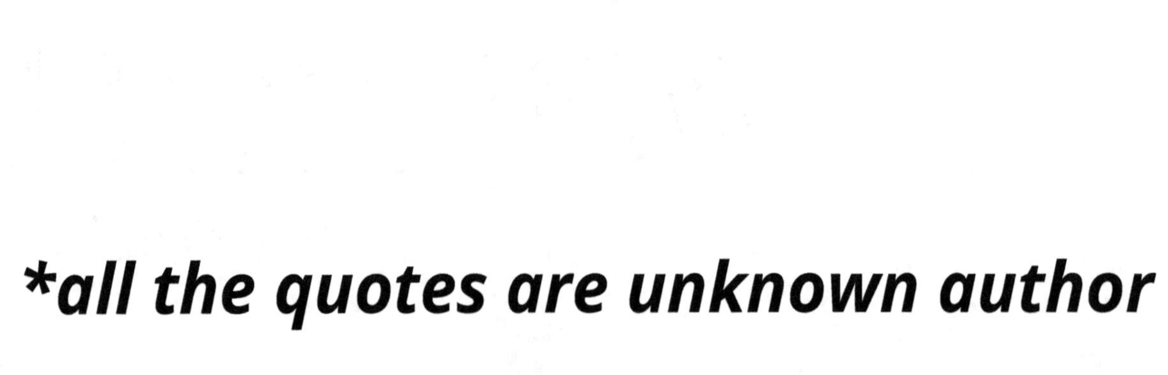

*all the quotes are unknown author

If you enjoy this
book at all, a quick
review on Amazon
would
really help us!